The Value of Friends

void

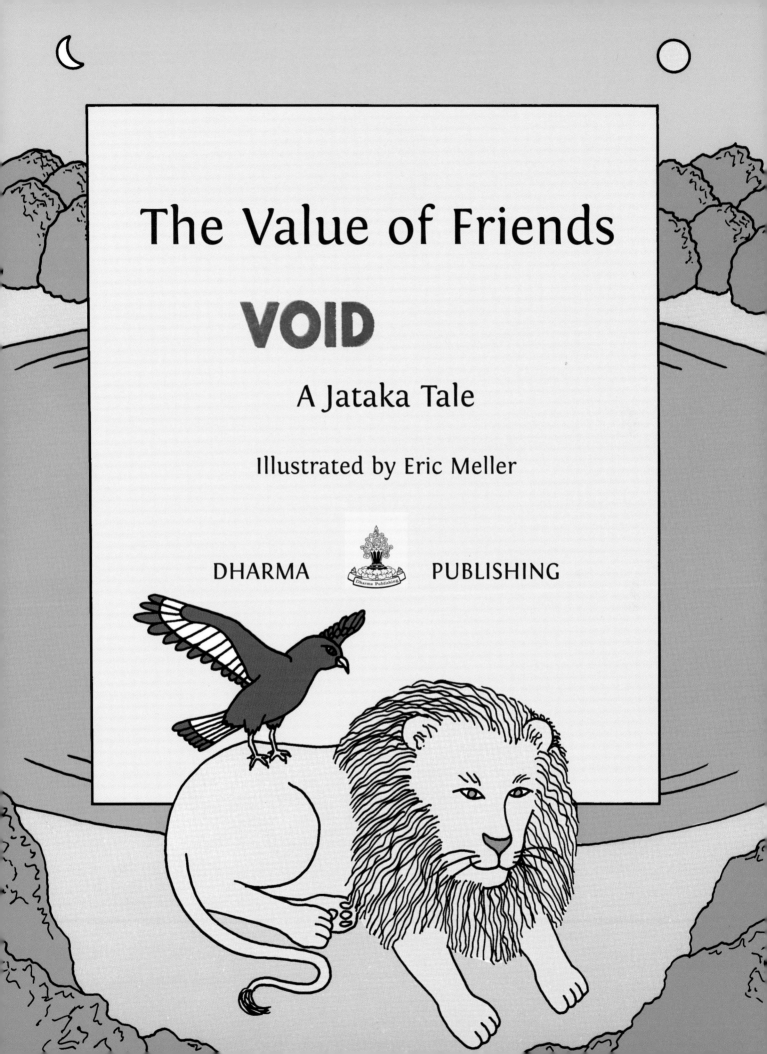

The Value of Friends

VOID

A Jataka Tale

Illustrated by Eric Meller

DHARMA PUBLISHING

First published 1990

Second edition 2009, augmented with guidance for parents and teachers

Printed on acid-free paper

Printed in the United States of America by Dharma Press
35788 Hauser Bridge Road, Cazadero, California 95421

9   8   7   6   5   4   3   2   1

Library of Congress Cataloging-in-Publication Data

_____

The Value of Friends: A Jataka Tale; illustrated by Eric Meller

(Jataka Tales Series)
Summary: A family of hawks is made aware of the value of friendship when their friends the osprey, the lion and the tortoise save them from hungry country folk.

Jataka stories, English. [1. Jataka stories]
I. Meller, Eric, ill.   II. Series
BQ1462.E5V35   1986   294.3'823   86-24164

ISBN 978-0-89800-493-9

Dedicated to children everywhere

Once upon a time in the far-off land of India, there was a lake in a forest, not far from a village. On the northern shore of the lake lived a Lion, king of the beasts; on the east an Osprey, king of the birds; on the south a male Hawk and on the west a female Hawk. In the middle, on a small island, lived a Tortoise.

One day the male Hawk asked the female Hawk to be his wife. She thought for a moment and asked: "Do you have any friends?" "No dearest," he answered, "I don't." "Friends are important," she said. "I will marry you and be your wife, but first you must find some friends. In difficult times we may need friends who can help us."

The male Hawk wondered, "Who shall we make friends with?" His bride-to-be answered quickly, "Why, with the Osprey who lives on the eastern shore, with the Lion who lives on the north, and with the Tortoise who lives on the island in the middle of the lake."

The Hawks went to visit the Lion, the Osprey, and the Tortoise and they all became firm friends.

The young couple built a home in a tall kadamba tree on one of the many islands in the lake. Among its branches, they made a nest and in no time, the wife laid two eggs. Soon two baby Hawks cracked open their shells and spread their wings.

One day some villagers came to the forest hunting for food, but found nothing. Not wishing to return empty-handed, they took a boat out onto the lake, hoping at least to catch a fish. They came to the island where the Hawk family lived and lay down under the kadamba tree to rest. To drive away the swarms of mosquitoes that tormented them, they built a fire that made clouds of smoke.

Billows of smoke rose up through the branches, making the young birds cough and cry. One of the men said, "I hear baby birds up there! Quick, we will smoke them out and eat them for dinner." They piled more wood on the fire until the smoke became very thick. Frightened, the mother Hawk cried out, "Go tell the Osprey that our young ones are in danger!"

The father Hawk flew as fast as he could to the
Osprey, who was just settling down for the night.
"What is your need, my friend?" he asked.
"Oh, king of the birds," said the Hawk,

"To our island some hunters came
Hoping to fill their bags with game.
They built a fire right under our tree,
To catch our babies who cannot flee.
Dear friend, please come immediately."

"Fear not" said the Osprey, "I will come.
Go ahead and tell your wife:

For those who are true and wise,
friends always respond to their cries.
For your sake I will perform this deed.
Friends help each other in times of need."

When the Osprey arrived, the hunters were just
climbing up the kadamba tree. Seeing this, the
Osprey dove into the lake, drenched his feathers,
flew out and sprinkled water from his wings and
beak over the flames. The fire sputtered and went
out. The men, annoyed, climbed down, built
another fire and climbed up again. Once again
the Osprey dove into the lake and showered the
fire with water to put it out.

Over and over, the men rebuilt their fire and each time the Osprey put it out. When the mother Hawk saw that the Osprey was tiring, she told her husband, "Dearest, ask the Tortoise to come quickly so our friend the Osprey can rest."

The father Hawk flew off and found the Tortoise asleep. "Goodness friend, what is the matter?" she asked. "Please, dear Tortoise; our babies are in terrible danger:

"Perhaps I have been selfish in the past,
But I'm afraid that my children won't last.
Are you willing to come with me
To help our little ones get free?"

The Tortoise answered:
"Father Hawk, my best efforts I will lend,
I would do anything for an honorable friend,
For you I will perform this deed,
Friends always help in times of need."

Swimming to the bottom of the lake, the Tortoise swept up all the mud she could carry. She climbed onto the shore of the island, pushing the mud forward until it smothered the fire. Then she pulled her head and feet into her shell and lay very still. One of the hunters saw her and cried with delight, "Why work so hard to catch a few small birds? Let us roll over this large tortoise and have her for dinner instead!"

They cut down vines to make ropes and tied them around the shell of the Tortoise. But tug as they may, they could not roll her over. Meanwhile, the Tortoise began to move toward the water, dragging the men behind her. Then she slipped into deep water and swam away quickly. Determined to catch the Tortoise, the men held onto the ropes and were pulled into the lake after her. Finally they let go and swam back to the island, coughing up the water they had swallowed.

"What is happening?!" They looked at each other, bewildered. "First an osprey keeps putting out our fire and now a tortoise drags us into the water and tries to drown us. And still we haven't eaten a thing! Let's light another fire and catch those birds. A few scrawny birds are better than no food at all!" The mother Hawk overheard them and told her mate, "Sooner or later these men will harm our family. Go and find our friend the Lion."

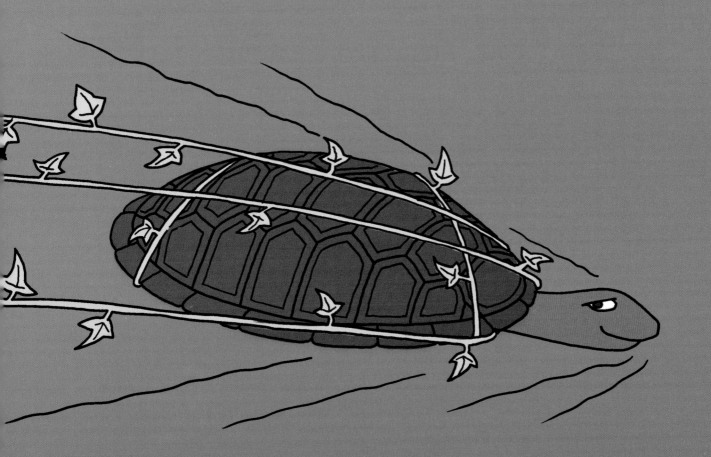

Once again the father Hawk flew off, this time to awake the Lion. "The sun has not even risen," he growled. The Hawk said:

"You are the Lion King and I am here
to beg for my family, trembling with fear.
Our little ones are in danger, good friend,
Your strength and skill we hope you can lend."

The Lion King stretched and roared:
"I will do what you ask, my friend,
Let us go and put your fear to an end."

When they saw the Lion swimming toward the island, the hunters were almost frightened to death. "The osprey put out the fire! The tortoise nearly drowned us! But now we are surely done for! This lion will completely destroy us!" They turned around and ran.

By the time the Lion reached the tree, all the men had disappeared. Then the Osprey, the Tortoise and the Lion joined the family of Hawks to celebrate their victory. The Lion spoke: "Always respect the bonds of friendship. Be sure to make good friends you can trust, and respond to their needs with a generous, loving heart."

Then each of the friends returned to their home.

The mother Hawk, looking at her little ones, said, "Through the gift of friendship, our children have been saved." To her husband, she sang:

"Dearest, see what friendship has meant.
Thanks to these good friends you sent,
Each one of us is safe and sound,
What better help could ever be found?"

They remained faithful friends for the rest of their lives.

PARENTS' AND TEACHERS' CORNER

The Jataka Tales nurture in readers young and old an appreciation for values shared by all the world's great traditions. These Asian folk tales were transmitted orally, memorized and passed from generation to generation for hundreds of years. The tales communicate universal values such as kindness, forgiveness, compassion, humility, courage, honesty and patience. You can bring these stories alive through the suggestions on these pages. Active engagement with the stories creates a bridge to the children in your life and opens a dialogue about what brings joy, stability and caring.

The Value of Friends

A far-seeing hawk is willing to marry her suitor on one condition: he must first make friends with other animals. The hawk couple makes friends with a lion, an osprey and a tortoise. The two hawks care for their young high in an island tree until hungry villagers try to smoke out the nest. Roused by the father hawk, each of their friends uses his particular skills at just the right time. The animals protect each other, save the young birds and honor their bond of friendship.

Key Values
Cooperation
Helping friends
Planning ahead
Loyalty

Bringing the story to life

Engage the children during the reading by saying: "We are reading a story in which a bird's nest is in danger. What do you think will happen?" Ask what will happen next when you turn each page.

- What did the female hawk ask the male hawk before she would marry him?
- What caused trouble for the hawks? How did they solve their problem?
- Who is your favorite animal in the story?
- How does each friend bring in different skills to save the hawks?
- How do you feel about the hunters? Why did they act the way they did?
- Have you ever asked a friend for help when you were in need?

Discussion topics and questions can be modified depending on the age of the children.

Teaching values through play

Follow up on the storytelling with activities that explore characters and values, and appeal to the five senses.

- Have the children color in or draw a scene that intrigues them. Then invite them to talk about what it means to them, exploring the key values.

- Construct and decorate masks for each character. Then have the children act out different parts of the story, playing the female and male hawk, the osprey, and the tortoise. Have the children speak in the voice of the character.

- Bring up a difficult or challenging situation that is going on in the child's life. Using the drawings and masks, ask questions such as: "Who might be able to solve this problem; the tortoise? Or the lion?"

- Have the children retell you the story in their own words; ask them to explain what motivates the villagers.

- Make up your own story about the value of friendship. Ask the children to give this tale a different ending.

Active reading

- Before children can read, they enjoy story telling and love growing familiar with the characters and drawings. You can show them the pictures in this book and tell the story in your own words.

- By reading the book to the children two or three times and helping them to recognize and understand words, you help them to build vocabulary.

- Children love to hear the same story over and over, with characteristic voices for all the animals.

- Integrate the wisdom of the story into everyday life. When the children leave someone out of their play, remind them of the value of friendship.

- Carry a book whenever you leave the

Ganges River

INDIA

house in case there is some extra time for reading.

- Talk about the story with your children while you are engaged in daily activities like washing the dishes or driving to school. Ask: "How could a group of friends work together on this problem?"

- Display the key values on the refrigerator or a bulletin board – at child's eye level – and refer to them in your daily interactions.

Names and places

India: A country in Asia. It is the source of many spiritual traditions and the background of most of the Jataka tales. The Jatakas clarify the workings of karma and illustrate the relationship between actions and results.

Kadamba tree: In India this large tree is common and used to be considered holy.

Osprey: A large sea bird, reaching 24 inches in length with a 6 ft wingspan. Also known as a sea hawk.

We are grateful for the opportunity to offer the Jataka tales to you. May they inspire fresh insight into the dynamics of human relationships and may understanding grow with each reading.

These adaptations of Jataka tales are for children aged three to eight

JATAKA TALES SERIES